M000190171

DECONFLICTION

Deconfliction

Katharine Harer

fmsbw

San Francisco, California

© 2021 Katharine Harer

All rights reserved

ISBN-13: 978-1-7329439-8-8

The poem "memory that floating petal" appeared in the author's previous collection *Jazz & Other Hot* Subjects (Los Angeles, CA: Bombshelter Press, 2016); "The Migrant Caravans" and "Hope's Trick" appeared in *Sin Fronteras* #24, 2020; and Rattle.com featured "Brett Kavanaugh Does the Dishes" on October 21, 2018.

Cover artwork by Johanna St. Clair

Author photo by Apolinar Elias Lopez-Carrasco

San Francisco, California

For the Hilly Galz Poets

memory that floating petal

I want to thank the dark world
I was looking for a sign
thought I wasn't good enough
not fucked up enough
for art

twelve or thirteen
no one home
I fed a paper napkin into my mother's typewriter
banged on the black plastic keys
hammered my way in

CONTENTS

BULWARKED IN THE QUOTIDIAN

Two eggs cooked in butter, wheat toast, black tea.
You can do it. You can keep this machine set for living.

Rain fills the mud puddles fuller
slopes of good land wash away.

Change a light bulb. Install batteries in the smoke alarm.
Hang your mother's favorite Picasso, the print
you gave her years and years ago
when nearly everyone you loved was still alive.

You can do this. You can push back the flood.
Fry up some bacon. Make a salad.
Buy large serious houseplants.
Scrape the stains off the toilet bowl.

•

I am perfectly
imperfectly
alone
even the dog ignores me

I holler at the wet trees
for attention

they sway
in the rain
inside their own hunger

their beautiful
refusal.

•

1

The forest is still. Nothing moves
and if it does, I don't see it
caught on my side of the window.

Why am I sitting in a chair in a room
in the middle of their world?
Stands of tall brown trunks
sky-thick canopies.

INSTRUCTIONS IN A DARK TIME

Bend to the mechanisms of flowers
the sparkle of a dropped earring
on the street.

Avert your eyes from steaming coils of shit
human or dog
fascinating as they are.

Look instead at a woman's pale blue sweater
the curve of her breast the sky
with its daily blessings of light.

Turn away from the hungry man draped over a sawhorse
the group of human vines
clinging to the dry fountain.

When small children like butterflies
appear on warm days fluttering in scattered circles
notice their flashing life.

Don't think about where they'll be
in ten years
or twenty.

There's a stone in your shoe
fish it out
hold it to the light.

HOPE'S TRICK

Despair so easy. Hope so hard to bear. – *Thomas McGrath*

Hope is exhausting
an uncooked egg
easily shattered by too much enthusiasm.

It asks for a commitment. A show.
Just do it! Ride the ice-slicked hill to the bottom
risk breaking your neck.

Hope grows on hope. Like yeast
give it a pinch of sugar it will usually rise
which leads to bread.
But you know the story with bread.
Every day you need more.

Hope makes you feel less smart.
You have to give into it blindly, squinting
afraid to look.

It takes courage to defy the shitty odds
the way my son used to juggle eggs
grinning madly.

IN DEFENSE OF WEEDS

Weeds blossom. Madly. Unscrupulously.
We fear they'll strangle our better flowers
the ones we pay for at the nursery.

Stronger than pretty hot-house petunias more confident
eager to drink the rain, weeds survive the drought
with green bravado, laughing their way through our yards
choking out the serious flowers with their hilarity.

My body used to be a weed, a wild and hungry green blade.
I loved its hungers, its uncouth weediness. The weed
of my body craved dirt and wet smells, sun and the sure
touch of a gardener's hands, my own or someone else's.

When I pull up weeds their roots hold on hard
fighting before they give in, refusing to leave
their dark home. A small victory for the tidiness
of my garden, for the petunias twirling in their fancy
little-girl dresses. For the weed that was my body.

THE HOSPITAL FOR BROKEN DOLLS

She was broken again.
I couldn't screw her arm back into its socket
not even with the sharp end of a butter knife.
I wrapped her in one of my father's red cotton handkerchiefs
buckled her onto my roller skate and took her in.
I forgot to comb her golden hair.

They admitted her without asking her name
which made me sad.
The Doll Doctor said some pounding might be necessary
and rolled her away into a small white room.

When he was finished she wasn't the same.
She still had her real arm
but it wouldn't bend up or down
it stayed outstretched asking for help.

Back home I wound her long hair into a French roll
and pinned it with bobby pins.
I gave her a bath in my mother's cut-glass bowl
put her to bed in a cigar box padded with cotton balls.
We never talked about the operation.

THEN

I grew up in the fog belt
alone in the house
the floor heater blasting.
I felt myself whole and strange
an embryo of the possible
a small dot in a landscape of maybes.
I checked my face regularly
in the bathroom mirror.
My mother and my grandmother
were there beside me in the glass.
My pretty mother always tired from work.
My sturdy grandmother pointing out
the pimple on my chin
my bangs that needed cutting.
They told me with their faces
where mine was heading.
I hair-sprayed my hair and frowned.
Popped the pimple and bled.

HOUSE

When I came back I was never there
not until yesterday when I remembered
not until I saw my old room the orange
corduroy bedspread Frances sewed for me
and smelled the toast still sitting in the slots
of the toaster. Then I knew I'd been far away
and that I wasn't like other little girls.
H-Bombs exploding on my street
Johnny Mathis on a shelf of LP's
his maple syrup voice.
I'd been gone so long I forgot
which key opened the door.

MY REAL FATHER LOOKS BACK ON HIS HISTORY

I was tall and skinny
an Irish vagabond.
Guitar on my back
I took off for Spain.
I was handsome enough.
Called myself a Marxist.
Talked about the down-trodden.
Took pictures, black and whites,
mostly of her. She was a handful.
Beautiful, the way Jewish girls can be.
Complicated. Dark inside
and out. We had a baby,
a girl. I didn't stay
long enough to know her,
the baby. Her mother didn't
want me around is what I thought.
She cried all the time – not the baby,
her mother. I couldn't take it.
Left and looked like a bad guy.
Alright, I was a bad guy.
That baby. She's writing
about me. If I don't know
what I am, how could she.

PETALUMA

My grandparents made a bed for me
on their back porch. I watched
the lights of cars on the highway
the points of stars in the black sky.

I was three
carried here by my mother
away from my father
his memory leaching from me.

Feral cats, small dark ghosts, gathered
at the side-door for food, never for touch.
My grandmother put out saucers of milk
they wouldn't drink when we watched.

I wanted to keep them and name them
but they didn't need me.
I sat on the living room floor making families
out of buttons collected in a golden can.

My grandfather took me to the chicken house
and placed a baby chick in my cupped hands
it trembled inside its feathery weight
its small breakable bones.

He stroked it with one finger
and told me it would grow big and round
and he would sell it to Henry from Chinatown
and everyone would love the tender sweet meat of this chicken.

I stretched out my hands to my grandfather
to take the chick and he put it back
on the wooden floor where it joined
the humming pale yellow cloud.

I knew then I didn't belong
to the shivering chicks or the rangy cats.
I belonged to the highway and the stars.
I belonged to my grandparents. I knew that.

ANTIDOTE TO THE CURRENT OBSCENITY
2017

He touched her with his mind
and she touched him with hers.
She thought she started it
but he thought they did it together
his touch slow and steady
hers quicker.
They danced through summer
then cooled in fall, thoughts turning
to holidays, family, dinner.
When she overate she couldn't touch him.
He felt her cold hands
taking leftovers from the refrigerator.
Winter came and left
and after the terrible rains
when hillsides washed away
and basements flooded
she began to touch him again
with just the tips of her fingers.
She started with his hair, his neck
little finger strokes.
He was in her garden
waiting.

BRETT KAVANAUGH DOES THE DISHES

Brett's hands are elbow deep in soapy water
washing the plates, one by one, attacking
the slime of egg yolk, coagulated bacon grease.
Brett rinses each plate but he can't get them clean
he rubs his fingers back and forth
across their china faces but the filth
holds on. This isn't Brett's job, the dishes,
but he volunteered this Sunday morning
while his wife and daughters
sit at the breakfast table newspapers
spread open under their eyes.
They look at each other questioning.
This isn't Brett's job doing the dishes
but he made his tight-mouth face
and walked purposefully to the bright white
sink in the bright white kitchen. Brett runs the
hot water squeezes bubbling soap on the sponge
and scrubs. His family watches from the other side
of the breakfast nook with its potted
plants, unflinching sunlight.
Brett stacks each gleaming white china plate
in the dish drainer in a shining line.
He grunts and tackles the heavy skillet
a pool of white grease stuck to its dark bottom.
He scrubs and scrubs and scrubs and scrubs and scrubs.

THE MIGRANT CARAVANS

after a poem of the same name by Alejandro Escude

We are the cruel animals and we are the sky
thick with birds and bombs.

We are the rain and we are the moon
shining like an unspent quarter.

We are jangled skulls damaged hearts flower pickers dog-cradlers.

We wait on our side of the street for the caravans to arrive
make soup set the table bring hydrangeas into the house
more deeply red as they die.

We are the cruel animals
with arrangements of flowers on our tables.

We are the sky
full of ash and light.

POEM STARTING WITH A LINE BY JUAN FELIPE HERRERA

In a bed made of leaves and torn handkerchiefs
homeless dogs settle for the night
nervous with hunger

none of them will lift their heads
to howl at the round white moon
none will lick their paws clean
or rub the brambles from their faces

or listen for the whistle
that will call them home

PELAGIC WATERS
from Sandra Anfang's "Song of Salmon"

Whales mate and cry
deep down the ocean's
throat

burst the skin
of the Pacific

breach and fall
slap and fade

to a horizon
we almost see

watching
from our rock

to see
just to see

the eye of the underworld
winking

SUGAR MOUNTAIN

you're leaving there too soon

the sky's clean
as though nothing
ever happens there

the small Christmas cactus
about to explode
into blossom

overnight
its flat uneventful leaves
sprouted buds

pale pink bullets
aimed at life

IN THE DIRTY LIGHT OF LOSS

This light is knife-point-sharp
so bright I shut my eyes
but it pries them open
it makes me look

You're in the fun house mirror
disfigured, wrong
I run outside
to Laffin' Sal, cackling,
hideous

You're walking beside me
so bright I can't take my eyes off you
your brain dark and soft
your eyes preposterously blue

We sit in the sun
eating hospital cafeteria salads
and you almost make sense

(title from a poem by Frank O'Hara)

AND SO IT IS PAST ALL ACCIDENT

To find again and again inside ourselves
love – small, low-watt LED-bulb love.

Despite the bad habits of our tongues
the unkindnesses. Despite ourselves.

Camilla, turned six, reminds me not to put
the wooden whistle we found on the street in my mouth.

"Don't" my little neighbor says firmly,
kindly. I set the whistle in a patch of grass at our feet.

Camilla smiles, nods her approval,
takes off barefoot for home.

                    (title from a poem by William Carlos Williams)

DRAFT DELIBERATION

I command everyone I love to hold still.
We call that dinner.
The dishes clatter in the sink
and everyone's gone. Even me.
We call that the continuum.
Life's roadside stops:
a cup of coffee, a meal, a toilet.
We look down the highway
where we've been, where we're going
and it seems sensible.
Like there was a plan.
Like the whole sweeping thing was under our control.
But it's just one moment after another.
Drops that swell and burst.
I'm in one now, black pen scratching on blue lines.
Another swollen drop about to break,
water running down a mountain.

I command goodness to rule the day
but these drops have their own logic. Cancers.
Disappointments. Long falls. Robberies.
I left the door unlocked. I let them in.
I'm permeable.
Now I can't get rid of them,
their scuff marks on the rug
their hands opening drawers.

I command everyone I love to stay in place so we can be safe.
A swollen drop breaks and spills into another drop
and another and I can't hold anyone here. Not even myself.
People break in. Others break out and leave us on this side.
It's all spilling, running down the mountain.

The robber's marks will fade.
I'll make dinner and everyone will leave.
I'll leave too.
Water running down the mountain.

LINGUISTICAL

poem beginning with a half-line from Grace Marie Grafton

In the ropy arms of sex I quibble
calibrating fingertips, checking messages.
I free the pigeons from their rooftop cage
stroking their feathers as they fly, words
hooked to my sighs. Why are there so many
people in this room? Dripping water tap
of thoughts pings down, dissolves into moist
night smells. I practice banishing everything
but this. Muscles firm and flesh warm. Incendiary
rocket play of stars, stars with new names
I can't pronounce. Even words must go.

FRANCISCO ALARCON
February 21, 1954 - January 15, 2016

So now we're dying we poets who scrabbled for work
to buy the time to sit and wait for a poem
like a voice through the veins of a phone
we hope we'll hear hope will speak to us
who drove miles and miles in our beaters
to read to 15 or 20 if we were lucky
half of them there for the wine or hiding from the cold
who cheered us silently later, much later,
stirring their soup or lying in their beds
when something we said rose up inside the square walls
of their apartments and they said to themselves
that poet got it right, she got it right.

We drink and talk and salute one another
or forget to. We mean to. I meant to salute Francisco.
He had to die to remind me that I knew him and liked him
his poems, his large smiling face.
One time he forgot to come to a reading
I made for him but I forgave him, or if I didn't I do now.
I'm sorry for holding on to something so small, Francisco,
when you are so large, grinning like a child
thick with heart.

ALBERT TAN

Where are you this winter morning
are you standing on a city street
snow sailing out of the sky
landing on your shoulders
your upturned face
you're a man now, 43 years old,
what are you thirsty for in this life

All around you men and women hurry past
trying to beat the snowfall
rushing to find a heated room
but you stay where you are, palms up,
letting the sky collect in your hands

Later, you'll tell your children the story of snow
how it comes to us when we need it,
how each small wet flake is a falling star
you'll open your big hands and show them
where the snow visited you today
and they will open their small hands
and practice what you taught them

THE FIRST SKY IS INSIDE YOU

I'm looking for the sky
inside me. I know it's there
but I can't find it.
I look at the other sky for help
the one outside Judy's window,
the sky that keeps my body tethered
to the ground for which I am grateful.
I am not ready to float away
from my feet and hands
my hungers and tears.
I ask my breath to lead me
to the sky inside me.
We listen together for an inkling
of space, an opening
of the fist of self.

(title from a poem by Li Young Lee)

HOPE SPRINGS ETERNALLY

after a composition by jazz pianist Helen Sung

She starts on the high raindrop keys
descends to the tough, growling ones
the drummer rat a tat knocks
at the door, the sax player slides
into dimly-lit spaces inside his horn.

I'm at the bar with a whiskey,
deep-fried shrimp, a bartender
who refills my glass and listens.

On the way to the club the taxi driver
talks about death because I ask.
He says: God is here and we can feel him.
God decides when we die.

I don't say it out loud, but I don't feel him.
Maybe I don't know how.
Now that people my age are dying
people I've loved, could still love
I want to leave all doors open
let the Hindu cab driver
teach me something I can use.

We have an expiration date, he tells me, like milk
and once milk goes bad, you can't change it.
God decides, he repeats softly, firmly.

I think he can feel how out at sea I am
so he adds: Praying helps. And being kind.
I know about being kind. It's the only thing I know.
But what about the expiration date, I want to say.
Does God change his date stamp if we pray?

But I don't say anything.
He's in a zone, a zone I wish I could enter,
and I don't want to lose his prayers.

VOICE MESSAGE
February 2020

Katharine,
I'm talking to you
I see you're wearing my fuzzy gray sweater
the one with the hood
good, I'm glad you can use it.
I miss you when I see you
wrapped up in my sweater
writing at your desk.
You're aging, it's true,
but you look pretty good
you've got salt and pepper hair
just like me. You know,
I don't miss much.
I miss a scotch before dinner.
I miss dinner,
dancing to Fats Waller
the parties, the picket lines.
But everything, Kat,
is so much worse now.
We tried to fix it, but we failed.
I'm sorry we left you with this.
Sure, there were always assholes
but now they're running the world.
How did things get so bad?
Don't bother answering.
I know. I really do know.
I'm your mother
I lived through The Depression
and two wars, no three wars,
maybe more, probably more.
We lived through Hitler,
Mama's friends with blue numbers
on their arms.
You know, I think we're made
for trouble. We must be.

How else did we survive so long?
We're also made for dancing
in the kitchen before dinner
in the living room with the rug
rolled back.
Dance for me, Kat,
pour yourself a little cocktail
and dance.

REVERSAL OF FORTUNE

I'm happy to say you were wrong.
What you thought was true worried me
but it isn't so.
You were wrong when you said we don't have birds.
Birds come here. Right here.
Maybe not the loud mobs you grew up with in Rochester
in leaf-crazy trees drained of snow primping
for spring. Ours are different trees, less manic
and the birds here are quieter, more self-composed.
I hear them knocking their beaks on the trunks of pines
piping their wind-up jewelry box songs
their bustles, their cries and squawks
the flash of a cobalt blue wing.

RAGGED VELOCITY

A pink geranium bud opens, petals spread wide.
Next to it, its closed counterpart,
blossom sealed inside green.
Maybe tomorrow. Maybe next week.
Maybe never.

The puckered skin on my arms.
My brother's failing spine.
Time's ragged velocity.
How to look it straight in the eye.
How to see it at all.

Can I have my way with it
out-blossom the blossom,
let my petals fall.

PURE SELF WITH DOG

I thought the others would be worried
about me but they weren't really.

There's a purity about this
a cleared place.

A space of self
white and clean.

On the sofa next to me
the old dog licks his paws.

Maybe this
is how to die.

HOW IT IS

Me here, you there, your there
a different day than my here.
Here it's that sun-faded time of dinner-making
the air cooler, the light edgy, expectant.

I'm chopping onions and thinking
about food and tastes and what you eat now.
I think you would like this dal
bubbling in the pot, its fragrance
of turmeric coriander ginger cumin.

There it's morning you're clanking your spoon
in your smoothie bowl, checking your phone,
making one of your famous lists, a habit you got
from me. Tropical rain hits the roof in big warm drops.

I want to save some of this beautiful orange dal for you
but even if I freeze it, it won't last long enough.
I chop cilantro leaves then stop to reach for my phone
to see if you've left me a message.

We'll sit down to dinner soon. You'll drive
to Uluwatu to check the surf.
Our phones are magical
but they can't carry your tight hug
across these deep seas.

A MAN'S REGRETS

He regrets the kind of father he is.
His son's unwashed hair and genital stink.
He regrets the sticky plates in the sink
nests of hair in the bathtub drain.

He regrets his wife telling him what to do
regrets not doing it and hating her
for knowing what he should do.
He regrets not knowing what to do.

He regrets leaving her in a crater
of memories and unpaid debts.
He regrets taking the stuffed animals
from their bed, the photos from the wall.

He regrets leaving their daughter
crying behind her bedroom door.
He regrets himself
his belly, his very breath.

4 AM
PGE Power Shut-Off, November 2019

I wake to pitch black
search the room for a flicker
of something I know
press the cotton sheet against my chest
rub the callouses on my feet together.

I sit up in bed half-expecting to see
the soft glow of the TV light from Alberto's house.
Philosophical Alberto
who walks the neighborhood
straight-backed and steady every day.

I look toward the yard of the family next door
imagine the kids popping up and down
on the trampoline
listen for baby Charlotte's cries
but there are no sounds.

My neighbors are asleep in their beds
the stars are still in the sky
the darkness is complete
unyielding
but it's mine.

COVID WITH ME

Co-live with me, I say to my dog,
and forget to say to my man
we are both busy in our ways these sheltered days
and when we're not we make up projects:
let's buy a new lamp so we can read side by side,
let's make mini margaritas, let's stop listening
to the news, let's not be so tired,
but we are tired because I'm betting
without any science behind me
that we're wearing out our adrenals
as we wait for the disease to get us
like an invasion of ants.

We're safe, we think. We set ant traps
at every entrance. We own a full box of rubber gloves.
We practice the art of not panicking after we panic.
We practice reading because we're too busy
to read. Busy with what? Ants.
The small and steady stream
that smell when you crush them.
I've seen them inside the cups of flowers
and that seems both right and wrong.
Just like this disease.

AUBADE TO A NEW DAY
Covid Memo #1

The bees have arrived
they're nuzzling the lavender we planted
the first week of shelter-in-place

They crawl and circle and rub their bellies
in the fuzzy purple blooms
drunks in an orgy of pollen.

•

We find wildflowers in the hills
skinny survivors of wind and rain
tough-stemmed and sinewy

I stick them in a glass of water
and they last, holding on tight
inside their shelter of green.

DEAR LARRY
Covid memo #2

I'm sorry I forgot about you
ten years passed, twenty, thirty
I didn't remember to remember you.

I see you playing your silver flute
in the tunnel in Golden Gate Park
your curly head bobbing.

Now you're disappeared,
unreachable.
I can't fix it with a phone call.

You thought you had the flu,
your neighbor said, a bad flu.
You died alone in your apartment.

Just you and your cat
and then just your cat
licking your cold cheeks.

MASKED
Covid Memo #3

I'm a cipher without a face
my stringy body forgets it's flesh
my blinking eyes
two stars of hot light

I do a funky dance on the yellow X
in the grocery rocking to Bob Marley
a wet Clorox wipe on the handle
of my shopping basket

A collective of cells
blood and beating hearts
we stay six feet apart
and try to find each other's eyes

Ponder the artichokes
sniff strawberries through bound noses
bandits, Zapatistas,
Halloween tricksters

A bottle of sanitizer
brandished in my hand
an unsanitary smile
rising inside my mask

PRECARITY
Covid Memo #4

I drive a few blocks from home
to run in the hills
a huge sign says: *Stay away. Residents only.*
I drive past the sign
trying to be invisible.

A local woman stands on her porch
arms across her chest yelling:
"You don't belong here!"
I keep driving.

A young mom pushes
her daughter in a swing
in their front yard
she's singing *the eensy weensy spider
went up the water spout.*

She dances her hands into
cheerful spiders, friendly rain.
I want to sing with them
wave and smile.

But I lower my eyes
and drive
into the green
forgiving hills.

TOUCH STARVED
Covid Memo #5

A warm breeze fingers her heavy uncut hair
the soft paw of her neighbor's cat
strokes the inside of her arm

touch as light as one 15,000th of an ounce
sparks a nerve launches a rocket
into the sky of her brain

all the doors
in her body swing open

she remembers the child
who sucked chocolate sauce
from her fingers

swimming in a warm lagoon in Mexico
ripples lapping like tongues
against her skin

she turns on the fan
stands naked in front of its spinning blades
trembles inside its imaginary hands

FOREST MEDITATION
Covid Memo #6

there's a forest in her mind
a lake with soft grassy banks
it's high maybe 8000 feet in the Sierras
covered with dark green pines
handfuls of forget-me-nots sprinkled in the shady spots
their blue faces and tiny yellow eyes
remind her she can rest in the forest's hands
she can be naked sitting on the grass next to the lake
she can slip into the clear cold water under the open sky
she can decide to stay as long as she wants
and the forest won't kick her out
or make her go home

I AM LOOKING. I AM HUNTING FOR IT...

The beauty of an almost-thing
the tight bud of a rose
unready to open
and the over-thing
browned petals of hydrangeas
refusing to drop
holding their round flower shapes
through the dark winter months

Often imperfect
a bruised mango on the ground
split open in the rain
rotting lemons in the driveway
bright and fragrant
black spots seeping

In every stray yard
and gutter-puddle
a spill, a splash, a star

(title from a quote by Vincent Van Gogh)

Katharine Harer, 2020

Katharine Harer is a poet whose verse has been published in six small press collections. Her most recent book is a volume of new and selected poems, *Jazz & Other Hot Subjects* (Bombshelter Press, 2016). Her poetry has been published in anthologies, literary journals and websites and in the *San Francisco Chronicle*, and she often performs her poems with jazz musicians. Katharine's nonfiction projects include interviews with women who played pro baseball, a travel/memoir about Pablo Neruda, and travel-inspired personal essays. Her essay "Delle Donne" appeared in *Best Women's Travel Writing #11.* Her labor journalism has received numerous awards from the California Federation of Teachers, as well as an international labor prize in 2017.

Katharine teaches English at Skyline Community College in San Bruno where she is Vice President and an Organizer for the college district teachers' union, and she teaches memoir, personal essay and poetry courses at the San Francisco Writing Salon. Katharine is the former Statewide Director of the California Poets in the Schools Program and former director of Small Press Traffic Literary Arts Center, and she has worked as a California Arts Council poet in residence in two inner city high schools in San Francisco. Katharine attended San Francisco State University and the University of Nevada, Reno. She currently lives in San Rafael with her husband, Bob, and their dog, Ozzie, where she tends an unruly garden.

THE PAGE POETS SERIES

Number 1
Between First & Second Sleep by Tamsin Spencer Smith

Number 2
The Michaux Notebook by Micah Ballard

Number 3
Sketch of the Artist by Patrick James Dunagan

Number 4
Different Darknesses by Jason Morris

Number 5
Suspension of Mirrors by Mary Julia Klimenko

Number 6
The Rise & Fall of Johnny Volume by Garrett Caples

Number 7
Used with Permission by Charlie Pendergast

Number 8
Deconfliction by Katharine Harer

Made in the USA
Las Vegas, NV
29 November 2023

81798296R00038